Before You Say I Do

Richard F. Myers

Copyright © 2015, Richard F. Myers

All rights reserved. No part of this book may be reproduced, stored, or transmitted by any means—whether auditory, graphic, mechanical, or electronic—without written permission of both publisher and author. Unauthorized reproduction of any part of this work is illegal and is punishable by law.

ISBN: 978-1-329-08598-5

Scripture quotations marked KVJ are taken from the
King James Bible

Scripture quotations marked NIV are taken from the
New International Version Copyright 1984 Zondervan
All rights reserved.

Two are better than one; because they have a good reward for their labour. For if they fall, the one will lift up his fellow: but woe to him that is alone when he falleth. Again, if two lie together, then they have heat: but how can one be warm alone. And if one prevail against him, two shall withstand him; and a threefold cord is not quickly broken.
Ecclesiastes 4:9-12 KJV

Dedication

This book is dedicated to my wife, Helen Marie. Without her help, internal treasures, support, commitment, and faithfulness to our marriage, this book would not be possible. Her steadfastness through the good and bad times stands as a shining example to what a marriage is supposed to become. Thank you for your years of devotion and seeing in me what only you and God could have seen. I love you and am proud to call you my wife!

Introduction

Your time has come ... you're getting married. What an exciting time for you both as you plan all the details of your upcoming nuptials. There are all the details of the ceremony, the wedding shower, the bachelor party, and the reception to be considered and planned. There is so much to do in the pre-wedding stage, but I want to share with you a few keys for *after* the wedding.

In the United States today, over 50 percent of marriages fail. Hopefully, with the seven keys I give to you as my wedding gift, you and your spouse won't be part of that number. By using and following these seven simple principles, your marriage will grow stronger with each passing year. You will be on a continuous journey of joy, laughter, fun, and adventure—and you will fully enjoy the life you have chosen to live together.

My wife and I have practiced these principles for the last forty-eight years—they really work. Our life has been full and rich; we're best friends and lovers, and more in love today than when we said *I do*. We know they work, and by sharing them with you, we pray that your marriage is blessed and fulfilled.

Congratulations!

Chapter 1

During your life together, you will have many opportunities to disagree. You will even have some times when you might fight a little. For most married couples, the first five years seem to offer the most opportunity for these disagreements. It is the time when you are learning to adjust to each other's natures. It is also the time when you discover each other's faults, fumbles, and failures (not to mention the baggage each brings into the relationship).

You will discover during these formative years—and I call them formative, as they set the course for the rest of your marriage—the likes and dislikes of your mate. You will also realize all the little things that agitate you, things that you never saw in your spouse before you got married. It's called the "discovery phase" of marriage.

Before you said *I do*, you only saw the things that attracted you to him or her. There's an apt saying: Love is blind. You'll discover the truth of that statement over the first few years of your marriage. You'll discover he doesn't always put the toilet seat down; he watches a lot more television than you thought; and he's not a Mr. Fix-It like your dad. He'll discover you aren't a very good cook; you don't do ironing; you like to shop a lot; and fast-food restaurants are your go-to when you don't feel like cooking or are running late or are just plain tired.

All of these little discoveries will eventually lead to some disagreements, if not downright arguments. As these distractions and disillusionments turn into frustrations, fights will erupt. Here is where the first principle of marriage survival comes into play.

Principle One

Don't Keep Score

As we engage in these disagreements—sometimes called "battles"—our human tendency is to keep track of how many times we've fought about an issue. We store up the issues in our subconscious so as to bring them back out as our big guns in the next battle. In fact, have you ever noticed when you do have an argument, you really don't listen to what your fiancé—or now your husband—is saying? Why is that? Because you're already building up your defense or rebuttal in your mind, ready to retaliate with the "big bomb" so you can win the argument.

If you begin to keep score of how many times your spouse did something, you will be declaring a winner and a loser. When we propagate that kind of thinking, we determine how many times *you* were the winner and how many times *your spouse* won. The fact of the matter is that *both* are losers. The truth is, when you have that kind of mindset, disagreements turn into arguments, arguments turn into fights, and fights turn into battles.

When you're operating in that mentality, you'll rebuke your spouse with this kind of statement: "You always —" or "You never —" (this is where you fill in the blank!). Here's an example. "You make me so mad because you *always* leave the toilet seat up." Or how's this one: "You *never* get what I ask you to get me when you go to —" (again, fill in the blank). "You're *always* buying (charging) something for yourself *every* time you —." Well, you get the point!

Why is this principle so important to your marriage being successful? Each time an argument is ended, it must be put to rest—dead rest! In chapter 2 I'll tell you in more detail how to do that, but for now let's concentrate on "never keeping score."

As I said before, keeping score determines a winner and a loser. Once the ratio of winner versus loser is solidified, it sets one individual above the other. We begin to determine who is the stronger, better, more educated, and even more desirable mate. When that happens, regrets begin to build inside one or the other. In some cases, a skewed perspective develops in both of you, and now a superior *attitude* begins developing in one of you. If not checked, you may start projecting this onto your marriage partner.

When we make the decision to *not* keep score, the temptations of superiority never gain a foothold. Truthfully, it's very easy to not keep score once you determine to not do so. And the easiest way to not keep score is to always remember that you are in this marriage for the best of you *both*. If you realize that the two of you joined together makes one strong couple then keeping score becomes moot. *The greatest benefit of not keeping score is that you become one.*

You marriage is so much more than the ceremony you had to be joined together. You said your vows, which formed a covenant between you, your spouse, and God. Your marriage is much more than that covenant alone. A true and loving marriage is *a covenant before God and a shelter and sanctuary for your passions/dysfunctions.*

When there is no scorekeeping, you are free to not only discover each other's passions and dysfunctions, but also to live together in a safe place where you may grow without fear of ridicule, rejection, or belittlement. And as the years go by, you will discover that you have become one—you're now sharing your life as a single-minded—yet individually unique—couple in love, enjoying life's journey together.

"So how do we keep from keeping score?" Go to chapter 2.

Chapter 2

We have now learned the first principle. It's designed to keep your marriage on track to be a fulfilling, satisfying, and loving experience. Although it was simple to state, the temptation to keep score will be great. To help you with this, I want to reveal the second principle right away. It will help you to eliminate scorekeeping.

Principle Two

I'm Sorry

Principle two seems so simple to say, but you will find it extremely difficult to accomplish at first. The principle of saying I'm *sorry* needs a lot more explanation in order for it to work effectively in your relationship. On the surface, it seems that the person who was wrong or who started the argument is the one who says, *I'm sorry*. However, that's only part of the principle.

The full effect of this principle only works when, after a disagreement, argument, fight, or battle, both parties (husband and wife) say, *I'm sorry*! It's not just the one who started it or ended it, or who was the winner or the loser. Both must say *I'm sorry* in order to make it work.

I know what you're saying to yourself right now. See if it isn't along these lines:

"But I *was* right. Why do I have to say I'm sorry?"

It's very simple, and it goes back to the first principle, "Don't Keep Score." By both of you saying *I'm sorry*, you level the playing field again. No one is deemed the loser or the winner. *I'm sorry* puts each of you back on the solid surface of equality. There's no winner or no loser; you are now both winners.

"Let me get this straight. He/she started this argument and *I* have to say I'm sorry?" shouts the common sense reasoning of your mind.

Yes! Yes, you do. Here's why. You may not have started it, but you participated in it. You had thoughts, comments, and feelings that were expressed, or at least felt. You may have even had your feelings stepped on, which brings feelings of rejection, belittlement, and probably some hurt. If those feelings aren't addressed quickly, they will begin forming a foundation on which your marriage builds. By both parties saying *I'm sorry*, you remove the bad building blocks in the foundation. It now makes a little more sense, doesn't it?

This principle also takes us to a new level in our marriage. When each person tells the other person *I'm sorry*, they're sending a very strong, important, and loving signal to their partner. When each person tells the other person *I'm sorry*, what they are really saying is:

"Whatever we just fought about is not as important as our relationship. In the scope of who we are together, and what we want to become, you mean more to me than winning this argument."

Wow, what a powerful message to send to your spouse. *Being the winner is not as important as being a couple.* Even if the things said to each other were hurtful, unkind, or unloving, you now have the opportunity to wipe them out of the equation of your future happiness. These things can no longer be festering sores constantly reopened every time a new difference or argument arises between you.

I'm sorry are probably the most powerful words to promote healing and hope in the marriage relationship. When each person sees the power of togetherness as greater than the power of winning, they will consistently reinforce, validate, and uplift their partner to greater heights and for greater things. When the *I'm sorry* is said from the sincerity of your heart, it becomes a catalyst to your spouse to work harder on the relationship.

I must confess something to you at this point. At first, as you apply this principle in your life together, it probably won't come from the heart. It will come from the mind, without the full support of the heart. You will probably do it, if you do it at all, because you read it in this book. However, "practice makes perfect"—remember that saying? It's especially true in this case.

At first, it will be more of an act of obedience because you read it here, but it may not be a feeling from the heart. Your mind will rebel when you know it wasn't your fault. But the more you desire your marriage to succeed and become the relationship you've always dreamed it would be, this simple principle will move from just in your head to down in your heart. As your spouse begins to feel that change, he or she will also desire their *I'm sorry* to be heartfelt. And I promise you, this will happen.

On some occasions, especially in the early stages of your marriage, the temptation will be to bypass this principle. It really is so much easier to just try to forget the issue, the argument, the disagreement, and move on. But the seeds of despair and internal separation and distance will be planted, and you will reap the harvest of those seeds later in the marriage.

In order to beat the odds of failure stacked against marriage, you must maintain a level playing field. You must always remember this is about being a couple and not a sole winner. It's about a loving, forgiving relationship that is growing into one beautiful couple.

In closing this chapter, I want to remind you of one important fact. Saying, *I'm sorry* means you're saying, "I forgive you and will forget this forever—and I'm asking you to do the same." No more "garbage dumping" from past arguments. No more *you never* or *you always* statements allowed. You've leveled the playing field again, and you're both on equal footing: forgiven, freed from any hurt, and back in a loving position for the benefit of you both. Now you can allow your love for each other to grow without any obstacles of resentment, bitterness, or superiority standing in the way. Wow! What a relief!

Now on to Principle Three...

Chapter 3

I want to start off this chapter by giving you the third principle right away. It's the key for surviving all the obstacles life throws against marriage. Here it is:

Principle Three

What's Best for Us

That's the principle, but we must expand it to understand it. So here's the full version of that simple statement.

Always make decisions based on what's best for us, not necessarily what's best for me.

In the first few years of our marriage, we must learn to readjust our entire thought process and way of living. For all of our single years we considered how we were going to take care of ourselves. We made decisions based on what was best for *me*. But now it's no longer just about me, myself, and I. It's about us, us, and us!

We started this book by defining marriage as a covenant before God and a sanctuary for our passions and dysfunctions. We learned that a marriage needs to be a place where both husband and wife have the opportunity to walk out their dreams, to fail and still not be rejected, belittled, or ridiculed. To help that process along we must develop the mentality that marriage is no longer about just me and my desires and dreams; it's about *our* desires and dreams.

I must tell you that this mindset will take the biggest amount of adjustment in the early stages of your marriage. Your life as a single person was completely centered around what was best for you as an individual. You had to make decisions based on self-protection, professional advancement, personal development, and your own pleasures. There was no one else to consider, even if you lived with your parents to this point. Sure, you may have had to obey house rules, but what happened out of the house stayed out of the house.

Now you have another person for whom you're responsible. You must take into consideration their dreams, their needs, their fulfillment, and their purpose. It can no longer only be about you. A successful and happy marriage requires a give-and-take relationship. It's called *compromise*. Living by "what's best for us" blends the two of you into one strong couple, able to survive the onslaught of life's obstacles. And it's not a fifty–fifty deal with each other; rather, it's each partner giving one hundred percent that makes this principle work for your good.

Living by "what's best for us" declares "we can out-love, out-give, and outlast all the obstacles life is using to attack me and destroy us." Isn't that powerful? Isn't it reaffirming there is hope that you will have one awesome, constant honeymoon for the rest of your lives together? This simple principle has made our marriage the most exciting, fun-filled, loving relationship anyone could ask for in this life.

But I must tell you it doesn't magically remove all obstacles.

The first thing you will realize when you begin living your life based on this principle is that not every decision will seem to benefit "you" at first. Sometimes you will have to leave your own level of comfort in order for your spouse to engage in his or her dream. Other times you will have to overcome disappointment in your spouse's bad decisions—and even in their failures. You may have to pick up the pieces of broken dreams several times before one achieves the desired goal. In the immediacy of life, that's a lot to ask of someone. It's also very easy to see how you would have done it differently, and not so easy to see how this benefits you personally.

However, it's never about the "immediate" in a long-term relationship. Even though it may not seem like you have any benefit immediately, look at the long term. By making the decision based on "what's best for us," you've reinforced your faith, trust, confidence, and love in your spouse. You've said to him or her, "I'll stand with you no matter what. And whatever the outcome, we'll make it work together."

If you got that message from your spouse, no matter what occurred, how would that make you feel? Invincible, right? You would feel there's nothing you and he or she couldn't conquer. Somehow, the two of you would overcome, become stronger, and grow closer together as you pick up the pieces and move on. Now are you beginning to see the long-term benefit?

Knowing that your spouse feels accepted, loved, and secure will put into him or her a sense of well-being and happiness. Who wouldn't feel happy knowing their partner is by their side, no matter what happens? Knowing the same consideration will be afforded you when you need it brings that same sense of security to you. And let's be truthful about it; when one partner is miserable, the other is too. And likewise when one partner is happy, content, and fulfilled, so is the other.

While you may not see an immediate benefit for you on the decision of "what's best for us," the long-term effect brings you happiness, security, and unexplored possibilities. This is so much better than living by a "what's best for me" mentality.

In our next chapter we'll explore a principle that will validate, reinforce, and constantly reaffirm your decision that the person you married is the person for your life.

On to chapter four…

Chapter 4

This fourth principle is a special one for my wife and me and has reinforced the strength of who we are individually and as a couple. This one seems so simple and is said so many times that in most cases it has become meaningless. Boys use it to get something from a girl that should be saved for marriage. Girls use it to get what they want or need, perhaps because of a lack of it in their home life.

You have probably used, or better yet, said it without ever realizing the impact and power of what you've said. So here are those three little words you've said to family, friends, boyfriends, and girlfriends:

I love you.

Am I right? You've said those words to many people, for all kinds of reasons. You've said it to parents who supplied your wants and needs. You've said it to family members to express connection in the clan. You've told teachers, friends, boyfriends, and girlfriends *I love you*, all with an expressed intention to gain, fulfill, or replace something needed in your life. But in a marriage relationship those words work differently and have a much deeper purpose. So let's state the full principle and not just the words *I love you*.

Principle Four

Tell Your Spouse at Least Once a Day, *I Love You!*

Everybody says *I love you* on an almost-daily basis to someone. But now that you're married, those words carry the power of your oneness. Those words said from the heart will reinforce your commitment to each other until death do you part. Those three simple words, said to a marriage partner, will realign their focus on the most important thing in their life: you, their spouse. So when you say that to your spouse, amazing things you don't even see are happening.

"Why do we have to tell our spouse every day we love them? They should know that, because I married them. And if I ever feel any different, I'll tell them."

Have you ever heard that line? I have. Husbands probably won't say those exact words, but they're probably thinking them from time to time—and it shows in their understanding of love. Washing his wife's car is, to a man, an expression of his love. To a woman it's a gesture she appreciates, but it's not received as an act of love. Giving flowers to a wife demonstrates love to her, but a man will never understood why that is love—it just doesn't compute.

We are made to be individuals who need constant reinforcement and validation. We need to be told we are loved, cared for, and thought about, and we need to know we are the primary interest in our partner's life. The "I don't need to tell him/her every day" reasoning doesn't fulfill a human being's basic needs. For now, just agree with me that saying *I love you* daily is an important principle in marriage so that I can show you the purpose and benefits of this principle.

First, let me ask you how you feel when someone you love tells you *I love you*. Doesn't it make you feel important, validated, wanted, needed, appreciated, and, most of all, part of the partnership? When we love someone we want it to be reciprocated. We want to know our love is appreciated and returned in like manner, which brings us to the first benefit of its daily utterance.

Every time you tell your spouse *I love you*, you reinforce the fact that they made the right decision when they gave their heart to you. You also place value on your spouse, which energizes them to work hard to maintain and grow the love relationship between you. You're telling your partner, "You have value to me and my life, and you're worth all the effort in growing our relationship together." Man! How cool is that!

You know what you're also doing? You're refocusing your spouse's attention on what's really valuable and important to them. There will always be temptations from the opposite sex facing each of you. There are many out there who do not value the sanctity of marriage; they'll hit on you without regard to your martial status. By telling your spouse *I love you* as they leave home, you refocus them on your marriage and give them the strength to rebuke, refuse, and overcome any temptation offered to them. It's like a vaccination against temptation. You're reminding your spouse every day the importance of what you have together.

As *I love you* becomes a powerful force against intrusions into your marriage, the words *thank you* have the power to reconfirm love. Thanking each other for the daily things you do for each other solidifies the value and importance of your partner in your memory bank. It becomes a continuous reminder of what each person's contribution is to the partnership, and it places a high value on the relationship. And when a relationship is valued, validated, and vaccinated, the chances of separation and divorce drop dramatically.

I love you and *thank you* are now powerful tools at your disposal to keep your marriage humming along in marital bliss.

Now on to the next principle, which will make it easier to invoke these two powerful expressions of love toward the spouse you love.

Chapter 5

Before we go on to this next principle, let's quickly review what we've learned so far. Our first principle was *Don't keep score*. Second, after an argument, both partners say *I'm sorry*. Third principle: *Always make decisions based on what's best for us, not necessarily what's best for me*. Fourth, tell your partner every day, *I love you*, and remember the words *thank you* are the acknowledgment of value after your partner has offered you an expression of their love.

Now that we have those first four principles established, let's jump into number five and discover a secret that will keep the love fires burning, long after the flame of attraction has dwindled. Here it is:

Principle Five

Maximize the Best in Your Mate and
Minimize the Worst

As the years go by, many of the physical attributes of your partner will fade. That six-pack you so admired on him will turn into a keg. That beautiful hourglass figure on her will turn into—well, you get the point. Those physical things change, but there are also some internal things that will change—and some that will never change.

Hopefully, the person you're marrying has depth of character, a personality that blends with yours, some vision, and a few dreams. Perhaps your intended spouse has set goals for the marriage, has a purpose for his or her life, and maybe even a plan as to where they want the two of you to go. Maybe they've even thought out how to reach those goals and how long they hope it will take. All those things are of great value as you analyze your future life together. But …

You're also going to find things about your spouse, once you begin the journey of life together, you never dreamed you'd have to face. You'll discover annoying habits, character flaws, unrevealed personality traits—and a few unfulfilled expectations.

There will be some baggage you never noticed carried into the relationship, or some qualities you thought you could change once you were married. You'll also realize that what you are getting in a spouse may not live up to the expectations you were hoping for in them. So what do you do?

You invoke the principle, *Maximize the best in your mate and minimize the worst*. Now the question becomes, "How do I do that?" Let me try to answer that so this principle is activated quickly in your marriage and in your future.

Remember this statement: *What is appreciated will be repeated.*

Did you get that? What is appreciated will be repeated (or reproduced). Do you now see the importance of saying *thank you* when your spouse does something pleasing and beneficial for you as a couple? By appreciating what was done through a verbal expression of thanks, you are allowing a positive experience, an act of love or a kind response, to be registered as a benefit to both marriage partners. Doing this maximizes those good things in your spouse that help develop a strong and loving marriage. When you or your spouse realize that something pleases the other, unknowingly you will work to not only repeat it, but also to develop it as a model for future actions. You will work on finding those things that make the marriage happy, peaceful, and joyful instead of stressful, frustrating, and agitating.

When we do apply the principle regarding our spouse's makeup (their character, nature, likes/dislikes, etc.), we begin to look for those things that positively affect the relationship. When we learn to maximize the good in them and begin to minimize the less desirable traits, marriage becomes sweet. How do we do that?

First, we identify what pleases us, uplifts us, comforts us, and offers us feelings of safety and security. Then we positively reinforce those attributes by appreciating (valuing), validating, and expressing what those things mean to you personally—every time your spouse does it. You may tell your spouse something like, "I was really touched when you held my hand in the store the other day. I felt like you were proud to be with me." Can't you just see your husband's chest puff out in pride? And don't you know he'll start doing that again, and again, and again.

"I want to thank you for the hours you put in at work to help us enjoy a better lifestyle. I really appreciate that!" Can you imagine how your wife would feel if you came home from work and said that to her? Do you also realize the motivation you just gave her to do it again because you took the time to appreciate what she did?

Let me make an important point here so we don't get a wrong mindset regarding the duties and responsibilities of marriage. In every marriage there are responsibilities required just to live in harmony: beds need to be made, dishes washed, houses cleaned, grass cut, and a host of other things requiring regular attention. Many times we fail to recognize these things as "acts of love," and we put them under the category of "obligation of relationship." We tell ourselves, "Well, she/he has to do those things to keep the house and family going." We categorize it as "obligations" instead of "acts of love." Let me make another very important point here as well. *The value of one's worth is determined by the validation of one's presence and contribution.*

Even though there are "obligations of relationship" in every marriage, when they are taken for granted, rather than appreciated, a loss of desire to do them ensues. I wash my wife's car not out of the obligation that it's dirty, but out of a desire to show her I value her and want her in a clean automobile as she rides in town. This obligation now becomes an expression of value and an act of love. The car washing just went from obligation to validation.

My wife and I never go to the store for ourselves without also picking out something little for each other. When one leaves the house, the one left home will stand in the door waving till out of sight. When we are in separate rooms, we will call out, "I love you!" Or, "You doing okay?" And we never leave home without a goodbye kiss; we never walk on the streets without holding hands; and we always try to do things that confirm and validate each other's value. And by doing these things, we automatically maximize the positive (best) and minimize the negative (worst).

You will be amazed at the change in your spouse's demeanor, attitude, and desires toward you when you validate their worth. Your marriage is now free to take risks of expressing love in not just the traditional ways, but in ways that validate each other's contributions. So say *thank you!* even for those things we call "obligation of relationship." Then sit back and watch the *best* of your spouse elevate itself above all those troubling little things that get on your nerves and tend to destroy a marriage.

Chapter 6

You're about to engage in the journey of a lifetime with a partner you're really just getting to know. You may or may not have good jobs, a home or apartment, one or two cars, or a host of other things. But what's really important is, "You're in love!" Life is now going to be full of joy, fun, happiness, and marital bliss. Right? Well, maybe.

Most of us enter into our marriages with great expectations, and after what seems like a very short time they have become unfulfilled expectations. After a year, maybe a little longer, we realize there are more have-nots than haves. As we live our lives together, we are amazed at all the things we need versus the things we have. We soon realize there are not enough towels when friends come; we need lawnmowers, rakes, snow shovels, bed sheets, pillows; and wouldn't it be great to have our own washing machine instead of having to go to the Laundromat?

When this realization becomes a revelation, we begin to take a serious look at our financial picture. We recognize that we could use more money coming into the house regularly. We also know that if we keep taking from our savings account (if we even have one), or from the wedding gifts that we were saving for a honeymoon, a vacation or a down payment on a house, we won't have anything left for a rainy day. So we begin considering how to earn more to take off the financial pressure, or so we can purchase those things that are now "needs" in our lives. At this point, conversations with our spouse go something like this:

"You know, if we just had a little more money, it would take the pressure off us, and we would be happy." Or maybe, "If we had more money, we wouldn't feel all this pressure, and we could enjoy each other more."

This kind of thinking will continue throughout your entire married life if not checked at the very beginning. There will never be enough money for us to do everything we'd like or have dreamed of doing. But we tend to believe that if we had money we'd be happy for the rest of our lives. Look, however, at the lives of many who have vast fortunes, and the belief that "if only we had more money" is proven wrong. What then is the perspective we need to accept early in our marriages so we don't wind up chasing fickle dreams, false hopes, and withered concepts? Here's where Principle Six comes into play.

Principle Six

Money Follows Happiness; Happiness Never Follows Money

I especially want to make sure you get this principle, because the entire world of advertising tells you just the opposite. From how to earn more money to winning the lottery, we are constantly bombarded by advertisers who show us and tell us if we have money we'll be happy. So many young people's ambitions are to become a celebrity, a movie star, or a sports figure so they can earn the big bucks. We are a society that believes having big bucks equals having happiness.

The problem with that belief is that happiness is a state of internal being, not of external excess. True happiness comes from life, relationships, and experiences, not from possessions, accomplishments, and success. There are many very successful people with vast possessions who are not truly happy. Many divorced, many sick, and many lying on their beds of affliction would trade all their money to be happy again.

Happiness will never be found in things money can buy. You really need to get that statement and this principle. Yes, it helps to accumulate things that make life easier, but you and I know people who have very little and yet are extremely happy with life. Why is that? Because they've found the things that can't be measured by their accountants, stock brokers, and financial advisors. They've found the joys of life—those things that produce happiness.

Hold a baby in your arms for any amount of time, and see how you feel. Try to remember what you bought ten years ago with all that money versus that vacation on a shoestring budget you took with the family. It's never the money aspects of our lives that take residence in our memory banks. It's always the time spent in intimate embrace or in conversation and our experiences that linger in our minds forever.

It's the face of a grandchild, the kindness of another human being, the song that helped us get through a difficult situation. These are the things that bring up those warm, fuzzy feelings—not how much money we have. It's the anticipation of a vacation with loved ones, the graduation of your children, the birth of your first grandchild that makes the heart sing. It's all those things that make life what it is: a journey that eventually arrives at the same destination for all of us—old age and the passing of one's life.

If you want happiness, forget about trying to get it by chasing after money. Grab hold of the journey set before you and your spouse. Create experiences, make memories, appreciate one another, and above all, make love your focus, joy your life spring, and happiness your eternal goal. Then, as those things fill your life with an indescribable happiness, money will surely follow—because *money always follows happiness.*

Chapter 7

As the years go by in a marriage, there is a familiarity that sets in between spouses. We learn each other's traits. We learn the likes and dislikes, the habits, the thinking process, and yes, the shortcomings, weaknesses, and failures of our partner. As we continue in our marriage we gain a broader perspective of who the other person is, as well as—hopefully—who that person will become. Some of it will be very pleasing, enjoyable, and loveable, while other discoveries will be—well, not so wonderful.

Each of us carries baggage into every relationship we enter. In marriage, that baggage is exposed more than in any other relationship. After a relatively short period of time, all our raw emotions, feelings, experiences, and history start to surface. We show the true depth of who we are through our daily life together. The temptation to *compare* may be impossible to resist.

We'll do this by evaluating our current relationship with previous ones. We make comparisons with other boyfriends or girlfriends, with what we could have accomplished without our current spouse, and what we have versus what friends, family, and even neighbors have. This seventh principle addresses making comparisons, and it is so important in the survival of two people in a marriage. So let's get to it and explore it.

Principle Seven

Appreciate What You Do Have Rather Than
Regretting What You Don't Have

In every marriage there will be a great temptation to find (and mentally dissect) everything that's wrong with the marriage instead of what's right with it. As humans, we seem to have built into us, or have been conditioned by our growing-up environments and experiences, to find fault with things. For some ungodly reason, it's so much easier to find fault with people and things than to see the good.

When we take notice of someone, what do we see first? Usually we spot what's out of place in their dress, hair, makeup, or demeanor. In conversation we find faults of speech, ideology, and beliefs. We make judgments of success or failure in our evaluations of people every day; usually we think they will fail more than succeed. Because we have this inner tendency to judge and evaluate, we may very easily adopt this mentality in our marriage. When we begin to see more things wrong than things right, we are on the verge of marriage destruction.

As you live your life together, you want to put all the odds of success in your favor. To do that, you must make a concerted effort to find what's right in your spouse, your children, your home, your job, your environment, indeed, in every area of your life. Whenever we make comparisons to what others have and we don't, we'll become discouraged, agitated, disillusioned, and feel short-changed. Now our problems really begin—and if we allow this kind of thinking to continue, what we have won't be worth fighting to keep and we'll eventually give up and quit.

Many people in marriages today have quit. They have focused so much on the negative aspects of the relationship that they've shut down, given up, and quit. They still live in the house and sleep in the same bed with their spouse, but inside (emotionally, mentally, and spiritually) it's over for them. The result of looking at what you *don't* have will always be a *What's the use?* attitude and mentality.

So how do we change that factor in our marriages? We must start looking at what we do have—and force ourselves to stop noticing, centering on, and dwelling on what we don't have.

Every one of us has habits, struggles, and experiences that have formed who we are today, thus creating baggage we bring into our relationships. As long as we dwell on those things, life becomes harder. But once we center on all the good things we have, our spirits are lifted, we become appreciative, and life gets better. Notice I said, "life *gets better*" and not "life *changes*." Life may not change one bit, but your perspective of it will.

Whatever we dwell on today will set the course for what we'll experience tomorrow. Therefore, if we concentrate on what's good in our lives, our family, our job, and our relationships, we will appreciate them instead of despise them. Appreciation also sets into motion a valuable principle: *What we appreciate will be repeated*. This is akin to one I'm sure you know: *What goes around comes around.*

Here's a little test to prove this principle. Pick something your spouse did for you that you appreciated. Tell him or her how much you appreciated what they did and how it made you feel. Then just wait. I can guarantee they will repeat it again and again, as long as you validate them for what they did and how much it means to you.

So let's engage Principle Seven. Let's start by looking at all the good things about your spouse. Let's concentrate on one thing that you really appreciate about him or her. Then let's add a second thing, a third thing, and so on until we've found enough of the good to outweigh the bad things we know are there. You might even want to write them down on a piece of paper. Draw a line down the center and place all the good things you find on one side. Then, when something pops up that troubles you about your partner, write that down on the opposite side. Now you have something in writing to keep you focused on what you do have in your relationship rather than what you don't have.

Are we ignoring the bad? No! We're just *focusing* on what's right rather than what's wrong in our relationship. We're counterbalancing all the junk that is so easy to see by refocusing on what is usually just taken for granted. Once we've done this with our spouse, move on to our children, our home, our jobs, our family, and our friends. Take each area until there's more power of good working for you than all the power of bad that rears its ugly head.

"Is this that positive thinking stuff that was so popular years ago?"

No! It's counteracting the bad with the good. It's a little secret that will change the entire dynamic of the household. It will change the atmosphere to a positively charged environment rather than a place you dread coming home to each day. Each member of the family will work unconsciously to bless, help, encourage, and love one another. You'll help each other grow into people of greatness—and it all starts by appreciating what you do have, not regretting what you don't have.

Chapter 8

When you began reading this little book, I told you there were seven secrets (principles) for having a successful and happy, long and enjoyable marriage. We're finished with the seven secrets, so this chapter is a free bonus chapter—and we all like free, right?!

I've actually saved this chapter intentionally without advertising it to see if you would make it this far. I've also kept this book short with the hope that you would make it to this chapter before you stopped reading. Pretty clever—or sneaky, depending on your perspective, huh? So knowing that you're at chapter eight, I'm impressed, because what you've demonstrated is that you really want your marriage to succeed. So do I! Therefore, I want to share one other thing with you before we experience the final *The End*!

I don't want to confuse you; this is not "secret eight." Rather, it's a foundational principle that will increase the odds of you and your spouse making it to the end of your lives together. If you apply this principle in your marriage, it will add a dimension that no other secret or person is capable of instituting. I'm talking about adding God to your relationship.

The Bible has a verse in it that establishes a truth for longevity of life as well as of marriage. It's found in the book of Ecclesiastes, chapter four, in verse twelve. Here's what it says: *And if one prevail against him, two shall withstand him; and a threefold cord is not quickly broken.* (KJV) The part I want to focus on is "a threefold cord is not quickly broken." One version of this verse says, *A cord of three strands is not quickly torn apart.* (NIV)

In life there are so many things that fight against your marriage. The entire purpose of this book is to give you secrets to combat them. While two of you joining together can become a strong bond, a bond of three creates even more strength, adding to the possibility of success in your marriage. Including God in your relationship is like adding a steel strand into two cords of rope, which gives you a cord that can withstand whatever life throws at you.

It is a well-known fact that God is actually three persons in one. Sounds confusing, doesn't it? But it's really simple. There is God the Father, who created everything. There is the Son of God, Jesus, who came to earth to be a savior for humankind, keeping us from going to hell by accepting Him as the Son of God. And finally, there is the spirit of God, which is called the Holy Spirit. So it's Father, Son, and Holy Spirit.

The Bible also says we are created after His image. So we also must be three persons rolled into one—which we are. We are created body (the physical person), soul (the intellect, will, and understanding), and spirit (the person you are forever and ever.) The spirit is the part that goes to heaven or hell. But as you know, we can't see a person divided into three parts. All three parts blend into one person, who interacts with other three-in-one blended people. Now, with all these blended people, trouble will surely arise. So, like God, we are created as three-in-one blended people to help us overcome (with more power) the obstacles of life we encounter on this planet.

When we look at the statement, *A cord of three strands is not quickly torn apart*, we see its foundation is based on three (strands) becoming one (cord). Three strands (you, your spouse, and God) become a strong cord that is not easily torn apart through life's daily struggles. God is there to talk to you, to help in your decision-making processes, to guide you, and to comfort you when there are no easy answers to what's happened to you. He also helps you carry all the burdens of life that humans on this planet Earth have to endure.

As you and your spouse share your lives together on the journey that's called "life and marriage," God becomes the shield, the negotiator, the interceptor, the intermediary, and the love doctor for the two of you. He comes to the aid of your differences; differences that could wreck another marriage. He's there for you in good times and in bad times, always standing by should you need to call out for His help. Doesn't that sound like a partner you'd want in your marriage?

I can only testify to you how much a difference He has made in our marriage. Helen and I have been married for over forty-eight years at the writing of this book. We're happy, full of joy, and still excited about each other and about what the future holds for us. Considering I'm seventy and my wife is sixty-eight, that's quite an accomplishment in the world in which we live today.

We have made God, through His Son, Jesus, the center of our life together. That seemingly hard decision—especially if you're a type-A, success-oriented personality like me—became the most important decision we made in our early years of marriage. It was a challenge to make the choice to put God at the center of our lives and marriage—and it seemed unnecessary, as we were doing fine on our own. But after making it, it seemed the simplest and best decision of our entire lives.

You may already go to church, you may already have a relationship with God and talk to him on a semi-regular basis. Good for you! Don't put Him aside or replace Him with your newfound love. Keep Him in the center of each of your lives.

If you don't have a relationship with God, I would urge you—no, I would plead with you—take the time; make the effort to reach out to Him. See for yourself if He's not everything I've just told you. See if He won't be there in every season of your life, just like the insurance policy you purchase for your home, your car, and your life. The only difference is that He will be with you forever and ever—and that's a really long, long time.

In closing this book I want to thank you for allowing me to share a small part of your life. I count that as an honor not afforded to many. I hope the secrets and principles I've shared with you will ensure you a long and happy life together. I pray the time that it took to read this little book was time well spent, and that the fruit of these pages will be reflected in your life together.

My final prayer for you and your spouse-to-be is that your life be filled with love, joy, purpose, success, peace, good friends, and—most of all—God.

Happy Marriage

For More Information about Richard Myers or to order additional copies of this book, Contact Him At:
  Richard F. Myers
  11 Crescent Blvd
  Millville, NJ 08332
  PastorRFM@gmail.com